Silk Ribbon Embroidery

Australian Wildflower Designs

JENNY BRADFORD

GREENHOUSE

Greenhouse
Penguin Books Australia Ltd
487 Maroondah Highway, PO Box 257
Ringwood, Victoria 3134, Australia
Penguin Books Ltd
Harmondsworth, Middlesex, England
Viking Penguin, A Division of Penguin Books USA Inc.
375 Hudson Street, New York, New York 10014, USA
Penguin Books Canada Limited
10 Alcorn Avenue, Toronto, Ontario, Canada M4V 1E4
Penguin Books (N.Z.) Ltd
182-190 Wairau Road, Auckland 10, New Zealand

First published by Greenhouse Publications 1988
This edition by Penguin Books Australia Ltd 1990

10 9 8 7 6

Produced by Viking O'Neil
56 Claremont Street, South Yarra, Victoria 3141, Australia
A Division of Penguin Books Australia Ltd

Photography by Malcolm Cross
Design by Deborah Savin

Typeset in Bembo by Abb-typesetting Pty Ltd
Printed in Australia by Impact Printing (Victoria) Pty Ltd

National Library of Australia
Cataloguing-in-Publication data

Bradford, Jennifer Margaret, 1936-
  Silk ribbon embroidery.

  ISBN 0 86436 178 5
  1. Embroidery. 2. Ribbon work. I. Title.

746.44

Acknowledgements

I would like to thank my family and friends who have helped to make the production of this book possible.

My son Terry for his patience in translating my hand written script to the word processor and his tolerance when I kept changing my mind!

To Lois Kinsman for her constructive criticism, constant support and encouragement.

Also Barbara Torkington, a longtime friend and talented artist in her own field of porcelain art. Her sharing of knowledge and its application to my own work have been invaluable.

Thanks also to all my students, without their interest, encouragement and desire to learn there would be little point in developing new ideas.

I would like to thank Melva McCameron for introducing me to such a delightful form of embroidery at the Sturt Workshops, Mittagong. I sincerely hope she will gain satisfaction from seeing the work of one of her students in print.

Most of all I thank my husband Don for drawing all the diagrams, his perceptive proof reading and constant help in so many ways.

Jenny Bradford
1988

Contents

INTRODUCTION   7

1   MATERIALS   9

2   WORKING WITH SILK RIBBON   13

3   STITCHES   16

4   THE FLOWERS   21

5   CHOOSING SUITABLE PROJECTS   27

6   MOUNTING AND FRAMING   30

7   HOW TO MAKE THE PROJECTS
    ILLUSTRATED   35

8   RIBBON AND THREADS USED FOR
    FLOWERS ILLUSTRATED   47

9   OBTAINING SUPPLIES   48

Introduction

Pure silk ribbon has been used through the centuries in many decorative ways but it is only recently that it has made a very welcome reappearance in the marketplace. As with all natural fibres it is beautiful to look at and a delight to work with. The wide range of shaded colours available make an exciting addition to the many varied threads already commonly used in embroidery.

Silk ribbon work is a lovely form of embroidery which is comparatively quick to do. The ribbon gives a three dimensional quality to the work not commonly found in other types of embroidery.

The beginner will be surprised at the simplicity of the stitches while the more experienced embroiderers will probably find the emphasis in the book on details such as the correct manipulation of the ribbon most helpful.

The aim of this book is to teach the reader the basic elements of working with silk ribbon and to familiarise readers with the subject, so that they can adapt the technique for their own projects. Those who wish to do so will then have the knowledge to develop their own ideas and designs.

There are other forms of ribbon embroidery which use different types of ribbon but the designs in this book are specifically for pure silk ribbon. Other ribbons are not sufficiently soft and pliable to produce the same results. This does not however mean that interesting ideas may not result from experimentation with other types of ribbon once the basics are mastered.

Owing to the three dimensional effect created by the ribbon some of the embroidered flowers are very delicate. This is not a hard wearing form of embroidery therefore care must be exercised in the choice of a project. There are however many ways of using it as can be seen by the suggested projects detailed in this book.

Patterns are included where necessary and readers should find the chapter on framing helpful as it has wide application.

1
Materials

RIBBON

All the designs in this book have been worked with pure silk ribbon. To my knowledge, there are no other ribbons available which are as soft and pliable as the silk. Substitution of other types of ribbon will result in much heavier work.

Silk ribbon is available in a wide range of colours in three different widths, 2 mm, 4 mm, and 7 mm. (Note: At present the colour range is more limited in 7 mm than the narrower ribbons.)

The ribbon is packed in 15 m packs but most suppliers sell it by the metre (see page 48 for suggested sources of supply and page 47 for a list of colours used for the flowers detailed in this book).

THREAD

Small amounts of DMC brand stranded embroidery cotton are used for stems and highlighting some flowers. Suggested shade numbers for threads required are listed on page 47.

NEEDLES

Several different types of needles may be used successfully with ribbon. I favour fine crewel needles for 2 mm ribbon and crewel, chenille or fine tapestry needles for the wider ribbons.

I first learnt to do ribbon embroidery with fine

tapestry needles but have found from experience that these can pull threads as they pass through the ribbon. Large eye, sharp pointed needles such as crewel or chenille, pierce the ribbon more cleanly. The eye of the needle should be long enough for the ribbon to lie flat when threaded and wide enough to make a hole large enough for the ribbon to pass through the base fabric easily.

Straw or millinery needles are recommended for use with embroidery threads as they are very sharp and there is no enlargement at the eye to distort the ribbon as you work. Suggested needle sizes:

2 mm ribbon — No 7 crewel
4 mm ribbon — No 6 crewel, No 24 or 26 chenille or tapestry
7 mm ribbon — No 20 chenille or tapestry
1 strand embroidery thread — No 8 straw/ millinery
2 strands embroidery thread — No 6 or 7 straw/ millinery

CHOICE OF FABRIC

The samples shown in this book have been worked on a variety of fabrics. Natural raw silk, silk shantung, silk organza, cotton batiste and velvet. An interesting watermark effect can be obtained by using silk organza over a plain fabric such as batiste or bemsilk lining. Try different coloured organza over the base fabric to create softer or stronger shading possibilities. Some even weave embroidery fabrics work well but these need a backing of voile or similar weight fabric to prevent the threads from distorting as you work. Soft polyesters are also suitable.

> Points to remember when choosing fabric

- That the fabric should be soft. Stiff, harsh abrasive fibres will shred the ribbon.
- The texture, weave and colour of the fabric should complement the project. For example the natural colour seeded raw silk used for the plaques provides a more appropriate background for most Australian wildflowers than silk shantung or velvet. In this instance I chose a fabric to complement my project. Conversely, in the case of the evening bag, I allowed the fabric to dictate my choice of flowers. Orchids have a rich quality that harmonises with the luxury of velvet. Thus a decision has to be made when embarking on a project. If the type and colour of the fabric is the major consideration then the choice of design should complement that fabric. If however the composition of the design is more important the choice of fabric must be made with that in mind.
- The weight of the fabric chosen is equally important. Thick fabrics are too bulky for small mounts, such as the porcelain box tops and jewellery (see section on mounting). Remember that dark coloured ribbons have a tendency to show through delicate pastel fabrics so extra care is needed with the back of the work.

FADABLE MARKING PEN

Make sure you have a fadable marking pen and not a water soluble pen. They can be bought from craft and haberdashery shops.

I find a fadable pen essential. Marks made with these pens are designed to fade after twelve to forty-eight hours. Although I have had students tell me that they do not fade away completely I have never found this to be so. I do however recommend that you use them very lightly so that the ink does not soak into the fabric too much. Only draw in the lines you will want immediately because they can disappear very quickly. I also try to confine my markings to areas of heavy stitching so that they will be covered anyway — just in case.

MAGNIFYING GLASS

Many people find it helpful to use a magnifying glass when doing needlework. Opticians usually stock quite a variety of them. Some have lights included and these are particularly good when working at night.

2
Working with Silk Ribbon

THREADING THE NEEDLE

The fibres of silk ribbon tend to separate as it is worked, it also loses some of its body and is harder to manipulate if overworked. It is essential that you use **very short lengths — a maximum of 25 cm (10 inches).**

The following method of threading the needle allows you to use every centimetre possible and ensures that the ribbon does not slip out of the needle.

Thread the ribbon through the eye of the needle and, holding the end that has been threaded push the needle through the centre of the ribbon about 5 mm from the end. Pull back on the long end until the ribbon knots firmly on the eye of the needle. (Try this method of threading the needle next time you thread elastic or ribbon through a casing).

> Thread a needle for each colour ribbon you are using so that you do not waste any ribbon by re-threading each time.

STARTING AND FINISHING

There is no way of avoiding ends on the back of the fabric with ribbon work. Start by pulling the needle through the fabric leaving a tail of approximately 1 cm on the back of the work. Hold this tail under your finger as you start and, if possible, pass the needle through this tail as you work the first stitch. If you prefer, a tiny back stitch can be taken if it can be hidden under the first petal.

To finish take the needle to the back of the work and cut leaving a 1 cm tail. When working some stitches such as bullion lazy daisy the ribbon can be threaded through the back of the work, but great care must be taken not to drag the stitches of the more loosely tensioned ribbon stitch.

> When starting new threads be very careful, if you come up through previously worked stitches or ribbon tails, that you do not drag the ribbon and alter the tension of stitches already worked.

Stems and embroidery thread highlights should, as far as possible, be left until all the ribbon work is finished, as this helps to hold the ribbon ends in place. Finally, trim ribbon tails where possible.

MANIPULATING THE RIBBON

This is one of the most important skills to learn when handling ribbon. It is essential to take the time to make the ribbon lie the way you want it. The ribbon has a tendency to fold or curl as it is worked and if this is allowed to happen stitches will not take up the shape desired.

> Make *spreading the ribbon* part of your routine when working ribbon and straight stitch.

SPREADING THE RIBBON

FOR RIBBON STITCH AND STRAIGHT STITCH
Every time you bring the needle up from the back of the work at point A, pull the ribbon taut, holding it firmly under the thumb or between the thumb and first finger of your left hand. Slide the needle under the

ribbon and back towards point A pressing the needle firmly against the ribbon as you go. This should flatten the ribbon out and ensure the edges are not curled over or under. Repeat if necessary. If the ribbon still does not flatten, turn it over and repeat; it may have twisted as it passed through the base fabric.

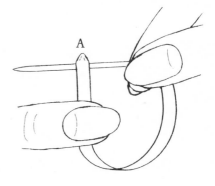

When winding the ribbon around the needle (as in colonial knots and bullion lazy daisy) make sure that the ribbon is not twisted but lies flat on the needle showing its full width each time it is wound around the needle.

When working loopy stitches (as in the Cooktown orchid) I find it helpful to keep a tapestry needle handy to slip into the loop as you pull the ribbon through. Slight upward pressure on the needle as you pull the ribbon down will prevent the ribbon from twisting and reduce the possibility of tightening the loops too much.

MAKING MISTAKES

It is very difficult to unpick misplaced stitches and virtually impossible to rework ribbon, so take care to get stitch placement accurate first time. However we all make mistakes and if you do find it necessary to unpick be prepared to sacrifice the stitches and ribbon in question and start again with new ribbon.

3
Stitches

As with all embroidery, perfection only comes with practice. It is easy to get quick results with ribbon but time and patience will be required to get your work just right.

As you read through the next pages I suggest that you start a sampler and practise the stitches as you go. Take a piece of fabric the size of a page in this book, then, using a permanent marker, divide it into twelve sections. Use the top two sections to practise each of the stitches. (The rest of the sampler will be used later for the flowers). Work each stitch several times varying the tension, the size of the stitches and the width of ribbon used.

SILK RIBBON STITCHES

Straight Stitch

Bring the needle up at point A. Spread the ribbon (see page 14) and push the needle down at point B, making the stitch the desired length and making sure all the twists are removed before the stitch is tightened.

Many different petal shapes can be achieved by varying the length of stitch and the amount of ribbon left in the surface loop.

Boronia, tea tree, wattle, correa and Cooktown orchid are all formed using this stitch in different ways.

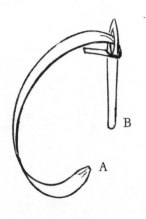

Ribbon Stitch

Bring the needle up at point A, spread the ribbon as before. Lay the ribbon flat on the fabric and push the needle back through the centre of the ribbon at point B. Pull the needle through to the back of the work very carefully as the shape of the petal or leaf depends on the ribbon just curling over at the tip. Tightening the stitch too much results in a straight thin stitch with no petal shape. The shape of the petal or leaf can also be varied by adjusting the tension of the ribbon between point A and B, before piercing the ribbon with the needle at point B, and by varying the distance between points A and B.

   Ribbon stitch is used for the leaves, the bluebell and in conjunction with other stitches for the waratah, correa and Cooktown orchid.

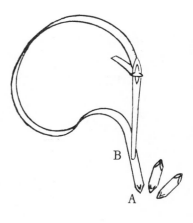

Bullion Lazy Daisy Stitch

This is a variation on the standard lazy daisy stitch (see *EMBROIDERY STITCHES*). A small bullion stitch takes the place of the usual anchor stitch at the point of the petal. The shape of the petal or leaf will depend on the length of the bullion stitch used.

   The secret of this stitch is to keep the ribbon taut at all times and not to be afraid to tighten it firmly before anchoring the bullion.

   Bring the needle up at point A, take it down again at point A and out at point B remembering that the bullion part of the stitch will extend beyond this point. Bring the ribbon under the point of the needle and wind it round the needle once or twice. Care should be taken to keep the ribbon flat around the needle and not allow the edges to roll. Lay the ribbon firmly to the base of the petal, hold in place gently by covering with the left thumb as you pull the needle through keeping it close to the fabric and in line with the bullion stitch. Anchor the bullion stitch by returning the needle to the back of the fabric at the very tip of the petal.

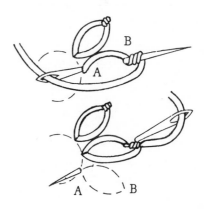

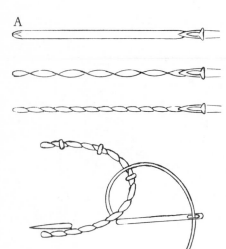

A

This stitch is used in the waratah, Sturt's desert pea, flannel flower and can also be used for leaves.

Twisted Ribbon Stitch

A very simple way of simulating a bullion stitch. Bring the needle up at point A. Roll the needle between the thumb and forefinger twisting the ribbon into a firm spiral. Take the needle to the back of the work to form a straight stitch or the twist may be couched into a curve by using a second needle with a single strand of matching embroidery cotton.

This is used for the gum nuts and could also be used for stems.

Colonial Knot (also known as the candlewicking knot)

This knot is larger and firmer than a french knot. It is attractive as it sits up well on the fabric. The ribbon (or thread) is wound around the needle in a figure eight.

Bring the needle through the fabric and with the left hand, pull the ribbon towards you. Point the needle away from you and pick up the ribbon with the needle, as shown in fig. 1, then swing the needle anticlockwise (as shown by the arrow) to face you. Pick up the ribbon again as shown in fig. 2 and turn the needle back to face away from you. Push the needle half way back into the fabric very close to, but **not** through, the original point of exit (fig 3). Hold the needle vertically while you tighten the ribbon round it. Tension the ribbon while you pull the needle carefully to the back of the work (fig 4).

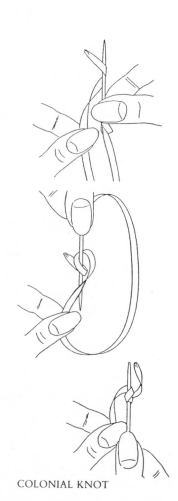

COLONIAL KNOT

The secret of neatly working all knots is to tighten the ribbon or thread round the needle as it is held in a perpendicular position when passing the needle from the front to the back of the fabric.

EMBROIDERY STITCHES

Pistil Stitch

Fig 1

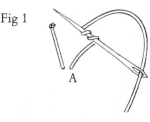

Used for stamens and worked in embroidery cotton. Use one or two strands as required.

Bring the needle up at point A. Pick up the thread twice around the needle (fig 1). Return needle to back of the work the required distance from point A pulling the thread taut around the needle as you do so (fig 2).

Fig 2

Modified Lazy Daisy Stitch

Fig 1

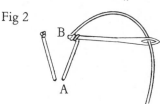

This stitch is used to outline the ribbon petals for the tea tree blossom. Bring the needle up on the left of the ribbon exit hole and take it down on the right hand side. Bring it out at the tip of the petal looping the thread under the point of the needle (fig 1). Pull the needle through the fabric tightening the thread only until it sits just round the ribbon petal. Anchor with a small straight stitch as the point of the petal.

Couching

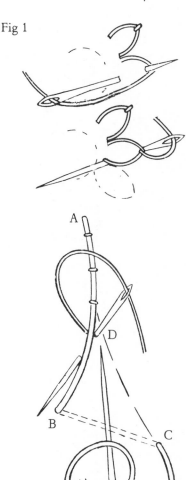

An excellent stitch for stems as it is easy to achieve a natural curve when working with two needles. Thread one needle with two or three strands of embroidery cotton. Thread a second needle with a single strand of the same thread. Using the thicker thread bring the needle up at point A and down at point B, bring it to the surface again at point C and leave this needle anchored in the fabric out of the way. Bring the second needle up close to point A and work a tiny straight holding stitch across the main thread. Work along this thread anchoring it at regular intervals curving the main thread as desired. Work a second stem from point C to D in the same manner. By using two needles you can adjust the amount of thread in the main stem as you go. The holding thread can be worked with a finer thread and is thus less obvious.

Bullion Stitch

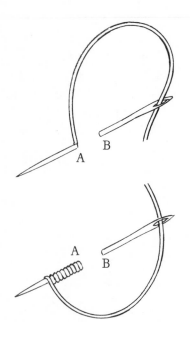

Using a single thread of embroidery cotton bring the needle up at point A, down at point B (about 4 mm away) and out again at point A. **Do not** pull the needle right through at this stage but wind the thread clockwise round the needle about fifteen times. Hold the wraps gently and pull the needle through. Tighten the wraps until they are even (the bullion will be slightly raised). Anchor the stitch by passing the needle to the back of the work at point B.

To work a bullion into a circle proceed as before but the distance between points A and B should only be enough to hold the thread firmly. Wind the thread around the needle at least twenty times, more if necessary, to form a circle of the required size. Anchor the stitch by returning the needle through point A instead of point B. Use a tiny couching stitch opposite this point to anchor the bullion stitch firmly into a circle.

4

The Flowers

Working the stitches you have now mastered into flowers is not a difficult process if it is followed through step by step. Have a clear picture in your mind of the real flower you are copying. When mixing flowers, their size is important for the arrangement to look balanced. There must be sufficient contrast between large and small flowers. Single flowers can be worked in a size to complement the article. The size of the orchids worked in the projects shown has been varied by using 2, 4 and 7 mm ribbons.

Use one section of your sampler for each type of flower and do not remove what you might at this stage consider to be a mistake. This sampler is worked as a reference. Looking at it in the future should remind you of how you did or did not achieve the desired result and it will enable you to avoid making the same mistakes twice.

You may also be surprised at how many so called mistakes can be the starting point of new ideas in the future.

The flowers are listed in order of difficulty. The measurements given and width of ribbon suggested are the ones applicable to the flowers on the large oval plaque. For a full list of the shade numbers used refer to page 47.

BORONIA

Yellow 4 mm ribbon   Brown 2 mm ribbon

- Using the yellow ribbon work one vertical straight stitch approximately 4 mm long.
- Using brown ribbon work one straight stitch on each side of the first stitch, fanning them slightly away from the stem. Work a third straight stitch directly over the original yellow stitch, commencing slightly above the first stitch and finishing just short of the yellow petal, to expose a yellow tip.
- Leaves are worked in ribbon stitch using 2 mm ribbon. Pull stitches firmly to give a thin spiky appearance.

WATTLE

Yellow 2 mm ribbon

- 1 vertical straight stitch, 2 mm long.
- 1 horizontal straight stitch to form a cross.
- 1 vertical straight stitch directly over the first stitch. Leaves are worked in ribbon stitch using 2 or 4 mm ribbon.

TEA TREE

Pink 2 mm ribbon

- Mark a tiny dot for the centre of the flower.
- Using straight stitch work five petals each approximately 2 mm long, evenly spaced around the centre.
- Outline the petals with a single strand of embroidery thread in darker pink, using lazy daisy stitch.
- Using two strands of pale green embroidery thread work a colonial knot for the centre.
- Leaves are worked in ribbon stitch using 2 mm ribbon.

CORREA

Deep pink 2 mm ribbon   Green 2 mm ribbon

- Using pink work one vertical straight stitch 4–5 mm long. Work one straight stitch on each side of the first stitch overlapping the stitches slightly.
- Using green work one very small ribbon stitch over the tip of each pink petal.
- Using a single strand of yellow embroidery thread work three pistil stitches for stamens between the petals. Leaves are worked in ribbon stitch using 4 mm ribbon.

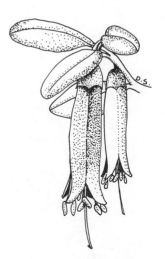

BLUEBELL

Pale or dark blue 4 mm ribbon

- Mark a small dot for the centre of the flower.
- Using ribbon stitch work five petals each approximately 4 mm long evenly spaced around the centre.
- For the centre work a bullion circle in green, using a single strand and winding it twenty times around the needle. Anchor it in place with a tiny straight stitch.
- Work a second straight bullion stitch in a single strand of yellow, from the centre of the flower to a point approximately 4 mm away, winding the thread fifteen times around the needle.
- Buds are worked with a single bullion lazy daisy, overworked with small straight stitches in green at the base.

GUM NUTS

Light brown 4 mm ribbon   Dark brown 2 mm ribbon

- Draw a gum nut the required size.
- Work one straight stitch in dark brown across the open end.

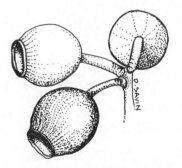

- With light brown and using twisted ribbon stitch, fill in the shell just inside the drawn line with straight stitches starting in the centre and working each side to correspond. Work two couched stitches around the dark straight stitch at the base. Work one long couched stitch around the top of the nut.

STURT'S DESERT PEA

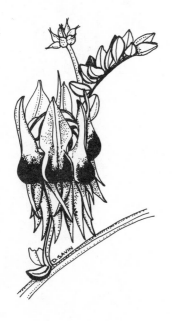

Bright red 4 mm ribbon   Black 4 mm ribbon
- Using bullion lazy daisy stitch work the centre petal of the top row first (the petals including the bullion are approximately 8 mm long). Work a petal on each side of the first one curving the bullion out slightly. Leaving approximately 2 mm gap work three petals for lower half of flower in the same order.
- Using black, work a small loose straight stitch between each of the top and bottom petals.
- Leaves are worked in ribbon stitch using 4 mm ribbon.

WARATAH

Dark red 2 mm ribbon
    The waratah can be worked in two ways. The centre of the flower can be filled in with either ribbon stitch petals or very small bullion lazy daisy stitches (wind the ribbon once around the needle for the bullion).
- Draw a dome shaped centre approximately 12 mm deep and 15 mm across the base.
- Start at the centre top of the dome and work the centre stitch, using either ribbon stitch or bullion lazy daisy stitch. Work a stitch on each side of the centre sloping them in towards the top. Continue filling in the dome shape overlapping each row and fanning the base of the stitches out adding more

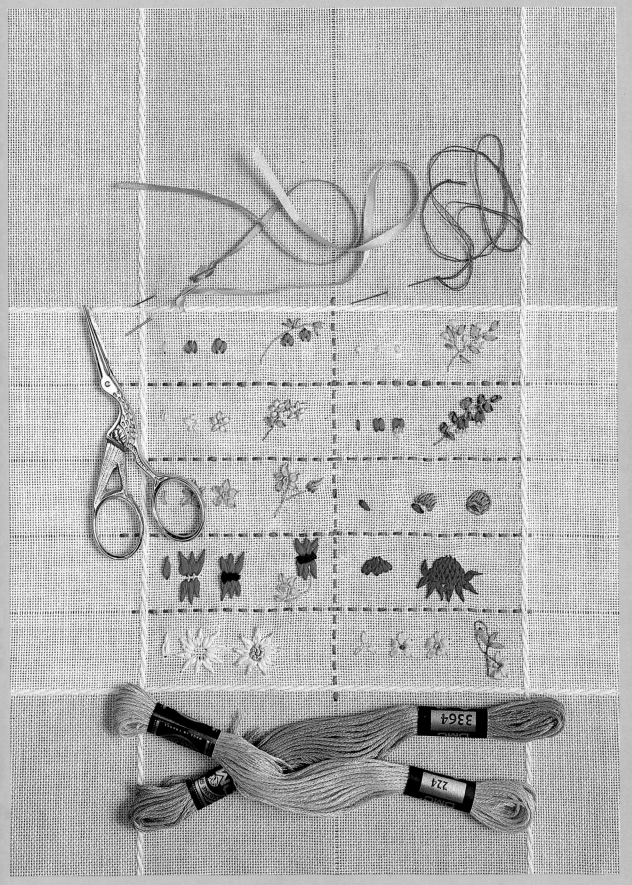

Become familiar with the technique by first working a sampler

This piece, which has each type of flower included, is in a wooden frame 15cm high

A great variety of projects lend themselves to this type of embroidery

Cooktown orchids have been embroidered on each of these pieces
but the ribbon width varies from 2mm–7mm

stitches to each row as required to cover the fabric completely.

- Work bullion lazy daisy stitches round the base of the dome, winding the ribbon three times for the bullion, and filling in the centre of each petal with a straight stitch.

FLANNEL FLOWER

Cream 2 mm ribbon   Green 2 mm ribbon

- Draw a small circle approximately 5 mm in diameter.
- Work nine to eleven bullion lazy daisy petals approximately 8 mm long (including the bullion stitch) around the circle winding the ribbon two or three times for the bullion.
- Fill in the centre with green colonial knots.
- Using green, work a back stitch over the tip of each petal. (Slipping a spare needle under the ribbon as the stitch is tightened can help ensure that the ribbon lies flat over the bullion).
- Leaves are worked in ribbon stitch using 4 mm ribbon.

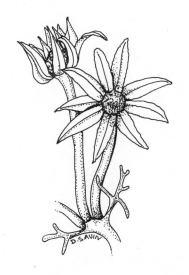

COOKTOWN ORCHID

Pink 2 mm ribbon   dark red 2 mm ribbon

- Draw a small circle approximately 1.5 mm in diameter for the centre. It will be easier to position the petals around this point if you consider it as a clock face.
- Work three petals in ribbon stitch each 4 mm long at 12, 5 and 7 o'clock. Using straight stitch work two overlapping petals 4 mm long between 2 and 3 o'clock. Repeat between 9 and 10 o'clock.
- Work a small straight stitch over the centre circle in deep red.
- Work the throat petals between this stitch and the

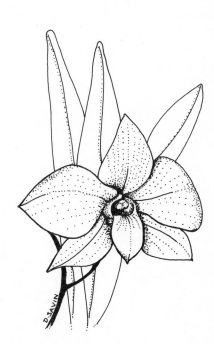

base of the outer petals. Bring the needle up at 10 o'clock and take it back down almost through the same hole slipping a spare needle through the loop. Tension the loop so that the ribbon flattens out and tighten the ribbon very carefully until there is a small loop sitting up from the fabric. Repeat the process at 2 o'clock being very careful not to pull the previous loop flat. Try to arrange these two petals so that they meet each other at the base of the outer petal at 12 o'clock. Position a third slightly longer loop at 6 o'clock.

- Leaves are worked in ribbon stitch using 4 mm ribbon.

5
Choosing Suitable Projects

The following information may assist readers in choosing suitable projects to display the art of silk ribbon embroidery. As it is a delicate and rather fragile form of needlework consideration must be given to factors such as assembly, laundering and handling of the finished work.

ASSEMBLY AND FINISHING

The back of silk ribbon work is impossible to keep tidy and therefore I recommend all projects be either lined or mounted. Care must be taken that the tails of the ribbon do not show through delicate fabrics and spoil the look of your work.

Ribbon work on heavier fabrics such as velvet can be sealed on the back with needlework finisher which is now available from needlework suppliers and craft shops. This finisher gives a clear pliable coating sealing the ribbons on the back of the work. It was used on the velvet evening bag to prevent the loop stitches on the orchids from being accidentally pulled.

Some stitches, such as bullion lazy daisy and straight stitch, are less likely to be spoilt by surface wear than others and they should therefore be used where this will be an advantage.

CLEANING

Samples of silk ribbon work were tested to assess their ability to stand up to cleaning.

Dry Cleaning

Some distributors of silk ribbon recommend 'dry cleaning only' on their labelling. The sample submitted for dry cleaning was a cushion cover worked on evenweave fabric. It was cleaned in fluorocarbon fluid and withstood the process very well. I stressed that the work was not to be pressed.

The results were excellent and pressing was not required due to careful handling.

Washing

Two identical samples of ribbon work on raw silk were hand washed in different solutions. The first was washed according to the manufacturers instructions in a special washing agent for hand washing pure silk and blended silk fabrics purchased from a local fabric store. The results were satisfactory but there was the faintest hint of colour leakage from dark red and dark blue ribbon.

This same sample was washed a second time in a strong detergent with unsatisfactory results. The base fabric went a little stiff and there was considerable colour leakage from the ribbon.

The second sample was washed in a good quality wool washing solution readily available in supermarkets. The results were identical to the first test using the silk washing agent, with a slight hint of colour leakage from the dark red and blue.

The best results were obtained by dry cleaning. Satisfactory results from washing will depend a great deal on the type of base fabric and the colour of the ribbons used for the embroidery.

PROJECT SUGGESTIONS

Your embroidery can be used to personalise a selection of items such as those in the Framecraft range. These are generally available from good needlecraft stores and some craft shops. The range includes porcelain, wood, crystal, gold and silver trinket boxes in a variety of shapes, colours and sizes. The mounting process is very quick and easy but, because of the three dimensional nature of the ribbon embroidery the clear protective disc provided must be discarded. See mounting information on page 30.

The wide range of cardboard mounts available for craft projects also present many possibilities. Ribbon embroidery can be used to decorate the fabric for covering these mounts before they are made up into the various items. No detailed assembly instructions are given here as these are readily available from other sources.

Jewellery projects are comparatively quick and easy to do. Suitable mounts are not always readily available and I find the most successful source of supply to be stockists of china painting supplies. The china discs sold for porcelain jewellery make an excellent base on which to mount your fabric (see Chapter 6). They are slightly domed which dispenses with the need to pad the mount and they can either be fitted into a metal surround or backed with suede for a neat finish. Some porcelain discs have a hole pierced to take a ring or similar finding through which to thread a chain. Provided you use a fine base fabric this is still possible. If china painting blanks are not used it will be necessary to cut accurate mounts in stiff card.

Ribbon embroidery can be used on various bags such as evening, lingerie or hosiery bags and jewellery holders. Coat hangers, decorative cushions and pot pourri sachets are also suggested. I am sure readers will be able to add many of their own ideas to this list.

6
Mounting and Framing

Successful presentation of your work can make all the difference to the end result. It is therefore something that should be considered when you are planning your project and not, as is so often the case, as an afterthought.

Framing can be a costly process but with careful consideration and planning the cost can be kept to a minimum.

I always recommend purchasing your frame first.

Square frames are easy as they can be made to fit the picture. However it can cost considerably more to have a frame custom made and besides it can be very annoying to find that had the picture been made a slightly different size it would have fitted into a standard size frame.

Oval and round frames are more limited in the range of sizes available.

I favour fabric covered mount surrounds for embroidery, as they are not difficult to make and they are more in keeping with the whole concept. The piece cut from the centre of the surround is used to mount the embroidery.

The diagram shows a cross section of how the frame parts fit together.

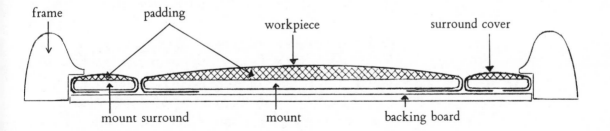

Mounts can be cut from plywood or stiff card. If you are unable to make these satisfactorily yourself a framing specialist will cut them from mattboard or stiff card. (Offcuts or damaged pieces can be used as they will be covered). Keep the piece cut from the centre to mount your work. Remember to cut it to allow clearance for the fabric. Mounts intended for fabric covered picture frames may be used if they are the correct size and if they have the centre cut out piece included.

Covering the disc which is normally padded, to fit into the centre of the mount surround, rather than placing the covered surround on top of the embroidery, has the effect of making the embroidery stand out so that it dominates the picture just as it should.

Embroidery is much easier to mount in this way, as stretching it around the centre disc gives an even tension, keeps the grain straight and eliminates all creases. Covering round and oval shapes is easier than square pieces in which the corners can be very bulky, especially if heavy fabric such as velvet is used. Oval or round plaques can of course be mounted into square surrounds and frames.

TO COVER ROUND AND OVAL DISCS

Make sure the disc has sufficient space allowed around it to fit after it has been covered with the fabric.

Remember that when the outside mount is to be covered as well, the space allowed may need to be up to 2 mm if a heavy fabric is being used.

Picture mounts cut from ply or card can be sanded down around the edge of the disc to adjust the fit.

Metal frames for china painting blanks and Framecraft boxes can not be adjusted and will not accept heavy weight fabrics.

Before commencing your project use the disc as a pattern for sizing the embroidery. Place the disc on the wrong side of the fabric, draw round it with a fadable marker and run a tacking thread round this mark to transfer the outline to the right side.

When the work is finished cut the piece out leaving ample turning allowance outside the tacking line. Using strong thread run a line of gathering stitches just outside the tacking line (about 1 cm on larger pieces, 5 mm on jewellery).

Pad the disc if required, using wadding or foam. *Lightly* spray the *disc* with spray adhesive, or apply a **very small** amount of adhesive to the disc, and stick the disc to the wadding. Then trim away excess wadding neatly round the edge. (Easier and quicker than trying to match up two cut edges neatly).

> Be very careful about how much glue you use. It is only necessary to use just enough to hold the wadding steady as too much will soak into the wadding and make it look lumpy and uneven when mounting is finished.

Place the disc face down on the wrong side of the embroidery, lining it up with the original tacking thread. Pull up the gathering thread, stretching the fabric over the disc. Check that the design is centred correctly as you can adjust it slightly at this stage. When satisfied that the work is correctly placed pull up the gathering thread tightly and tie firmly. You will probably find the tacking thread has been pulled to the back of the work due to the stretch of the fabric, but if it is still visible remove it carefully. Trim excess fabric where necessary.

TO COVER A MOUNT SURROUND

- Check the fit of the disc which should fit tightly when the surround has been covered. The amount of play will depend on the thickness of fabric to be used. Sand the edge if necessary.
- Cut a piece of fabric large enough to allow a good turning around the outer edge. Smooth the fabric out pinning to a board if necessary. Place the surround on the wrong side of the fabric lining it up with the straight grain of the fabric. Draw around the inside edge carefully. Remove surround and pad with wadding as previously described cutting the inner piece away with a craft knife.
- Cut out the inner piece of the fabric cover leaving ample turnings. Clip the turning at 1 cm intervals to the marked line. Replace the surround padded side down, centering carefully. Spread a line of glue around the back of the surround close to the inner edge and carefully pull turning through and stick to the back of the surround. Allow to dry making sure it does not slip out of place. When this is dry, use strong thread (dental floss is excellent) to run a gathering thread round the outer edge. Pull it up stretching the fabric and removing all creases from the front. Tie thread securely. This is less messy and gives more control over the fabric than trying to stick the outer edge.

    If these methods are used the discs may be hung as they are, after neatening the back by covering with fabric or card.

    Another alternative is to cover a backing board

which is the same size or slightly larger than the disc and surround. Stick the three pieces together and hang without a frame. The outer edge may be finished with a decorative edge of cording or lace.

7
How To Make the Projects Illustrated

PICTURES

The designs for the pictures illustrated in the book are given here but I hope that many readers will gain enough confidence to try their own ideas once they have worked their sampler.

The diagrams for the designs are intended as a guide for flower and stem placement rather than as a rigid pattern to be followed. If you find you do not have room to fit in as many flowers it is of no consequence; adapt and adjust the basic idea to suit your work. Interchange the flowers, try other combinations, change the colours — many of the flowers used here occur in a wide variety of colours.

For further reference and ideas refer to the numerous books now available on such subjects as china painting, gardening, Australian wildflowers, Australiana books and calendars all of which contain excellent colour photographs.

Many, including myself, have grown up with the idea that we are not artistic enough to create an original piece of work. However by observing pictures and artwork in any medium, ideas gradually form in relation to our own medium. It takes practise to perfect such ideas, but the results can be very satisfying.

Some points to remember when designing a picture

- Balance the design. The picture should not look too cluttered or fussy, neither should it be too empty. Approximately two thirds of the surface should be covered by the design and one third empty of design. This is a rule followed by china painters and one which I find works very well with embroidery.
- Balance the colour. Too much concentration of one colour in an area will unbalance the end result. I do not like using colours that clash next to each other, but colour is a very personal thing and Nature does not worry about such things in her distribution of flowers.
- When working small flowers it is interesting to note that, if the flowers are embroidered first they predominate over the foliage, however if the foliage is embroidered first it will have a tendency to dominate the design.

The pictures illustrated were all worked on seeded natural colour raw silk.

Flowers used are given in the key to the oval plaque. All diagrams are the full size of the original designs.

Method

- Using the centre disc (cut as described on page 31) as a template draw around it with a marker pen on the wrong side of the fabric.
- Run a tacking thread round this line to transfer it to the right side of the work before it fades away.
- If desired trace the design onto the fabric, preferably mark the main flowers as you go in case you decide to alter their positions slightly.
- Mount the fabric into an embroidery hoop large enough to take the complete design if possible.

When working the design be careful to keep well inside the tacking line as when the fabric is pulled tightly round the mount it can stretch and the tacking thread may well finish up towards the back edge of the mount.

> I find it easier to start with the largest flower, or at the point where there is the greatest mass of flowers in the design (eg. the waratah in the oval or round picture No 2, the flannel flowers in picture No 1 and gum nuts in picture No 3).

Work the flowers radiating from the starting point building the design as you go.

• Complete the design and mount according to instructions on page 30.

Set of Three Round Pictures

The originals are framed in round wooden frames 15 cm (6 inches) in diameter. Width of velvet surround is 23 mm (7/8″).

No. 1 — Flannel Flowers and Sturt's Desert Pea

No. 2 — Waratah, Correa, Wattle
and Boronia

No. 3 — Tea Tree, Gum Nuts,
Cooktown Orchids and Bluebell

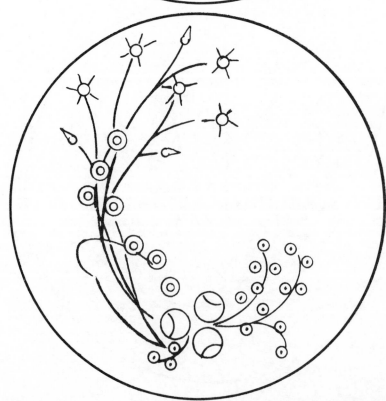

Oval Picture

The original is framed in an oval wood frame 20 × 15 cm (6 × 8 inches). Velvet covered surround 2 cm wide.

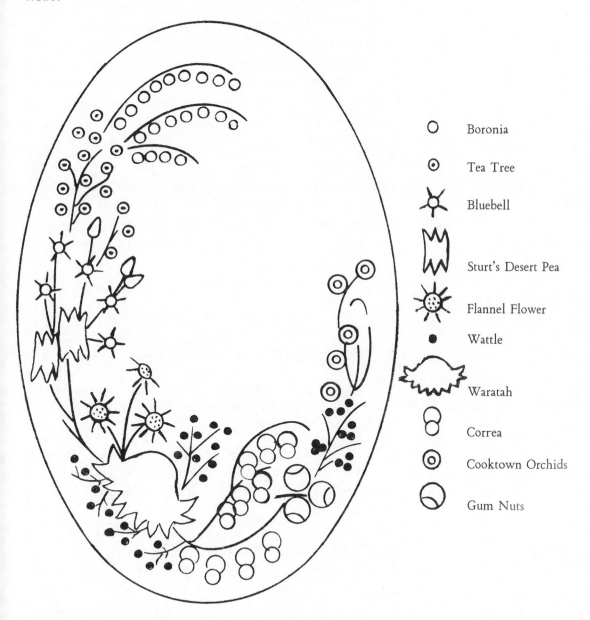

○   Boronia

⊙   Tea Tree

✳   Bluebell

     Sturt's Desert Pea

✳   Flannel Flower

•   Wattle

     Waratah

     Correa

⊙   Cooktown Orchids

     Gum Nuts

FRAMECRAFT BOXES

These come complete with all necessary pieces for mounting the work in the lids.

Follow the method recommended for mounting discs remembering to choose fine fabric as the push-in metal discs are very close fitting. Silk organza overlaid on swiss cotton batiste was used on the samples photographed. Take care not to work too close to the edge of the mounting disc, as the rim on the top of the lid encroaches on the design surface a fair way, especially on the small boxes.

Work the design in the same sequence as described for the pictures. In the case of the box pictured, a circle was drawn and the main stem couched into position. The flowers were then worked around the circle, leaves and stems joining the blossom to the main stem were worked last.

JEWELLERY

Follow the method already detailed for covering discs. If using commercial jewellery mounts I prefer the type with claws that fold over to hold the disc in place. It is more secure than gluing.

For pendants and brooches without frames cut a small piece of suede or similar fabric that will not fray (use the uncovered mount as a guide) sew on a pin if required and stick it over the back of the mount. For a pendant attach a jewellery finding to the top before gluing on the back cover. This will help to secure the finding.

As the colour plate shows, the basic designs given for the round pictures can be used for jewellery if they are scaled down and simplified by using 2 mm ribbon and omitting some flowers.

VELVET EVENING BAG

A small velvet purse closed by means of an embroidered stiffened velvet ring attached to the bag with narrow ribbon so that it cannot be lost.

Materials

- Piece of velvet, 24 cm x 34 cm
- Satin or silk for lining, 24 x 34 cm
- 40 cm x 15 mm wide belt stiffening
- 40 cm x 18 mm wide velvet ribbon to match or contrast with the velvet
- 30 cm x 3 mm wide velvet or satin ribbon
- Ribbon for embroidery

    The orchids on the pictured sample are embroidered with 7 mm ribbon on the bag and 2 mm ribbon on the closing ring.

Method

- Cut velvet and lining pieces according to the pattern on page 43.
- Embroider the required design. If desired the back of the embroidery may be sealed with a light application of needlework sealer or fabric glue.
- Place the bag right sides together enclosing the ends of the narrow ribbon in the seam 4 cm from the top of the bag. (Take care that the ribbon is not twisted in any way and that the loop does not get caught in the seam). Stitch seam.
- Pin the lining right sides together. Stitch the seam leaving an opening for turning on one side.
- Match the top of the bag with the lining right sides together. Stitch top edges together. Turn right sides out through the opening in the lining. Close the opening in the lining either by hand or machine.
- Press the top edges carefully.
- Closing ring. Cut the 18 mm velvet ribbon in half. Embroider with 2 mm ribbon a small design along 4 to 5 cm of one piece near its centre.

Silk Ribbon Embroidery

- Cut the belt stiffening in half. Form one half into a circle placing the ends edge to edge, using strong thread sew them together stitching across the join. Trim enough off the second piece until it will fit tightly inside the first ring (without the ends overlapping). Place the joins on opposite sides of the ring to form a firm circle and hold together with a stitch or two.
- Cover the ring inside and out with the 18 mm velvet ribbon.
- Oversew the top and bottom edges neatly with matching thread. (The attachment of the ring to the bag with the narrow velvet ribbon will cover the raw edges where they meet so there is no need to overlap them.)
- Attach the ring to the bag by sewing the looped end of the narrow ribbon firmly round the ring covering the point on the ring where the ribbon ends meet.

Pattern for Velvet Evening Bag

5 mm seam allowance on all seams

Enclose ends of narrow ⟶
ribbon in seam

> **Cut 2 — Velvet**
> **Cut 2 — Lining fabric**

Leaving lining open between
notches for turning

Design

CUSHIONS

As has already been mentioned in relation to pictures, rounded shapes are much easier to handle than square ones.

The method described here can be used to make any sized round cushion from a tiny perfumed sachet to a large cushion. The diagrams given for the round pictures can be used successfully as cushion designs.

You will need a piece of fabric large enough to cut one front and two backs, plus sufficient for the frill if it is to be made from the same fabric. (Allow 2 1/2 to 3 times the circumference of the circle for the frill.) On tiny pillows lace edging is the easiest to use. For larger cushions fine fabrics such as batiste, voile or silk organza may be cut double the required width and folded in half to give body to the frill and a neat edge.

A lawn backing should be used with fine fabrics to prevent ribbon ends showing through. Tack the two pieces of fabric together carefully before starting the embroidery. A zip closure is recommended for cushions 20 cm in diameter or larger.

Method

- Draw a circle the required size on the wrong side of the fabric and tack carefully round this line to give a guide line on both sides of the fabric.
- Work the chosen embroidery design.
- Cut out the pillow face allowing a 1 cm turning allowance outside the tacking line.
- Divide and mark the outer edge into four equal sections (by folding in half and then quarters).
- Prepare the frill. Divide and mark into four equal sections and join ends to form a circle. If double width has been allowed fold in half and press, matching raw edges.

Run two rows of machine gathering along raw edges. If using lace gather by hand or choose one that has a gathering thread woven into the top edge.

With right sides together and matching raw edges pin the frill to the cushion top at the four marked points. Pull up the frill to fit round the outer edge of the cushion top and tack in place carefully. Sew in place by machine using a long stitch 1 cm from the edge. (This stitching line should be over the original tacking thread.) For attaching a lace frill, position the edge of lace directly over the tacking thread and stitch carefully.

- Zip insertion. Cut two circles for the back, fold one in half and press. Open this piece out and lay on top of the second circle right sides together. The fold represents the centre seam, mark the length of the zip in the centre of this fold. Sew through both layers of fabric with a normal seam above and below these marks and use a tacking stitch where the zip will be placed. (fig 1)

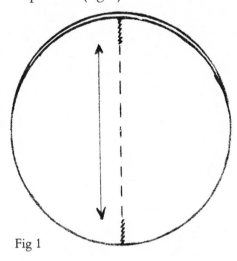
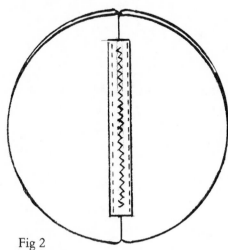

Fig 1   Fig 2

Fold the top and bottom pieces back to form two half circles. Lay them face down, iron if necessary and position the zip directly over the tacked seam, pin or tack as desired. Stitch the zip from the back (fig. 2), remove the seam tacking thread, open the zip slightly so that it can be fully opened to turn the pillow later.

- Place the pillow back, right sides together, over the front and frill. Tack carefully and stitch around the outer edge with the wrong side of the front face up, enabling you to use the stitching line of the frill as a guide for the seam. Trim seam. Open the zip and turn right side out.

- To make an insert. Cut two circles of firm wadding or lawn the same size as the original pillow. Sew around the outer edge using a 5 mm seam, leaving a small opening for turning. Turn and stuff firmly. Close opening. Insert into cushion.

- To finish small cushions without a zip. Sew backing on leaving a small opening for turning. Turn and fill. Close opening carefully by hand.

8
Ribbons and Threads used for Flowers Illustrated

Ribbon shade numbers are those used on the shade card for the Kanagawa brand of silk ribbon.
Embroidery threads are listed under DMC brand shades.
Because of individual variation in tension and size of flowers it is impossible to estimate accurately how much ribbon will be required for any one project. I suggest two to three metres of each of the main colours should be sufficient to work the practise sampler and the oval picture.

Flower	Width 2mm	Width 4mm	Width 7mm	Ribbon Colour	Kanagawa Shade No.	Stranded Cotton DMC Number
BLUE BELL	X	X		pale blue	125	Yellow — 743
	X	X		dark blue	45	
leaves	X			green	20	Green — 772
stems						Green — 3364
BORONIA		X		yellow	15	
	X			brown	77	
leaves	X			green	20	Green — 3364
COOKTOWN		X	X	pink	24	
ORCHID	X			pink	127	
	X	X		red	49	
leaves		X		green	20	Green — 3347
CORREA	X			deep pink	114	
	X			green	31	Yellow — 743
leaves		X		green	33	Green — 3362
FLANNEL	X			cream	156	Green — 3363
FLOWER	X			green	31	
leaves	X			green	32	
GUM NUTS		X		beige	66	
	X			brown	37	
STURT'S	X	X		scarlet	2 or 28	
DESERT PEA		X		black	4	
leaves		X		green	18 or 62	Green — 524
TEA TREE	X			pink	8	Pink — 335
leaves	X			green	20	Brown — 356
						Green — 772
WARATAH	X			red	49	
WATTLE	X	X		yellow	15	
	X			green	32	Green — 3364

9
Obtaining Supplies

Should you experience difficulty in obtaining the supplies mentioned in this book I suggest you contact the local branch of the Embroiderers' Guild, where a comprehensive list of supply outlets should be available, or the state crafts councils where a similar service is normally available.

Addresses of the main offices in each state are given below. Local branches of the Embroiderers' Guild can normally be found in the area telephone directory.

State Crafts Councils

Crafts Council of Tasmania
77 Salamanca Place
Hobart Tas 7000

Crafts Council of Central Australia
PO Box 85
Alice Springs NT 5750

Crafts Council of NSW
100 George St
The Rocks
Sydney NSW 2000

Crafts Council of South Australia
PO Box 17
St Peters SA 5069

Crafts Council of Queensland
GPO Box 1867
Brisbane Qld 4001

Crafts Council of Victoria
7 Blackwood St
North Melbourne Vic 3000

Crafts Council of the ACT
PO Box 720
Dickson ACT 2602

Crafts Council of the NT
PO Box 1479
Darwin NT 5794

Crafts Council of Western Australia
GPO Box D178
Perth WA 6001

Embroiderers' Guilds

Embroiderers' Guild of the ACT
GPO Box 146
Canberra ACT 2601

Embroiderers' Guild of Western Australia
29 Hubert St
Belmont WA 6104

Embroiderers' Guild of NSW
2nd Floor Cusa House
173–175 Elizabeth St
Sydney NSW 2000

Embroiderers' Guild of Queensland
149 Brunswick St Fortitude Valley Qld 4006

Embroiderers' Guild of South Australia
16 Hughes St
Mile End SA 5031

Embroiderers' Guild of Tasmania
PO Box 158
Launceston Tas 7250

Embroiderers' Guild of Victoria
170 Wattletree Rd
Malvern Vic 3144